Presidential

PET "TAILS"

BY Kathleen M. Muldoon

Perfection Learning®

BOOK DESIGN: Michelle J. Glass

DEDICATION

For Nancy Kroll, Kate Bohr, and Betty Minyard and their wonderful families

ABOUT THE AUTHOR

Kathleen Muldoon is a staff writer for a local newspaper in San Antonio, Texas. In her free time, she likes to write for children. She is the author of a picture book, *Princess Pooh*, and her work has appeared in many children's magazines. She especially enjoys writing fiction and nonfiction involving animals and also loves to write original and retold folktales.

When not writing, Kathleen enjoys reading, visiting the many historical sites in Texas, collecting old postcards, and playing with her cat, Prissy.

IMAGE CREDITS

Cover Images: Corel Professional Photos

Image Credits: AP/Wide World Photos pp. 39, 45, 47, 49, 50; ©CORBIS pp. 7 (top), 36, 41, 53 (bottom); ©Bettmann/CORBIS pp. 27, 30, 34 (bottom), 54 (top); AFP/CORBIS pp. 9, 53 (top)

ArtToday (some images copyright www.arttoday.com); Corel Professional Photos pp. 2–3, 3, 4, 5 (bottom), 6 (bottom), 13, 20, 21 (top), 23, 26, 33, 35 (middle), 54 (bottom); Corel.com pp. 8, 56 (top); Bureau of Engraving and Printing pp. 6 (top & middle), 16, 28, 34 (top), 40 (top)

Contents

Chapter One

Best Friends

Imagine you're visiting the president of the United States. You walk into the White House. You trip over a dog. The president shakes your hand. A parrot sits on his shoulder!

Many American presidents owned pets. They loved them. Some presidents even called them their best friends.

Long ago, presidents lived in the President's House. Later they lived in the White House.

Some early presidents had farm animals. Some had horses or goats. Others had chickens or cows.

Wilson

During World War I, President Wilson needed men to fight. So the White House gardeners went to war.

The president let sheep graze on the White House lawn. Their job was to keep the grass short.

Presidents had indoor pets too. Most were dogs, cats, or birds. But some were very different.

President Hoover owned two pet alligators. Sometimes they walked freely through the White House.

Hoover

President Lincoln had a turkey named Jack.

Roosevelt

President Theodore Roosevelt had many strange pets. He had a black bear named Jonathan Edwards. He kept a lizard named Bill and a snake named Emily Spinach.

He also had Maude the pig, Peter the rabbit, and Eli the parrot.

President Roosevelt's son with the family's pet parrot

Pets living in the White House have had great lives. Many people have taken care of them. Some pets have had fancy beds. Others have had their own rooms. President Clinton's cat, Socks, even had a white satin kitty house.

Presidents' pets get mail too. People write letters and send gifts to them. These people send pictures of their own pets.

Once President Kennedy's dog, Pushinka, had puppies. She received over 5,000 letters!

Some presidents brought their pets to the White House. They had these pets before they became president. Some added pets to their families after becoming president.

Visitors from other countries sometimes present animals to our presidents as gifts. Once a visitor brought lion cubs. Another brought a baby hippo! These kind gifts were donated to zoos.

Some White House pets become famous. A book was written about President Bush's dog, Millie. Other pets' pictures hang on White House walls.

Let's meet some of the pets that were American presidents' best friends.

Millie

Chapter Two

NELSON
George Washington's Horse

George Washington was our first president. He also owned the first presidential pets. But George Washington did not live in the White House. It had not yet been built when he became president in 1789.

President Washington, his family, and his pets lived in two different houses. The first was in New York City.

New York City was then the nation's capital. Later, the capital moved to Philadelphia. So did the president.

Even before becoming president, George Washington loved animals. He grew up on a farm in Virginia. He especially liked dogs and horses. He rode the horses and took the dogs along when he hunted.

As an adult, Washington had a farm called Mount Vernon. There he kept many animals. By the time he became president, Washington had 130 horses.

Washington was an excellent rider. Even after he was named general of the army, he rode horses into battle. He loved them all. But he had two favorites. He rode both horses during the Revolutionary War.

The first was named Blueskin. His hair was the color of gray stone. Washington liked him because he ran fast. He never seemed to get tired. Running was very important for an army horse.

But the other horse became George Washington's pet. His name was Nelson. General Washington rode Nelson into the important battle at Yorktown.

When Washington became president, he kept Nelson and Blueskin. Their work in war was done. They were free to spend their days grazing in a pasture.

Nelson's skin shone like a chestnut. He

was tamer than most horses. Sometimes President Washington went to the pasture fence and called, "Nelson!"

Nelson would stop grazing. He would run to the president. Then he would rub his head on Washington's arm.

People close to George Washington said that he treated his horses like family members. He cared about them very deeply.

The president hired people to work in his stables. One man was Gentleman John. He was in charge.

Gentleman John shared the president's love of horses. He liked to sneak Nelson extra treats.

But sometimes Nelson or another horse became sick or injured. Then President Washington took care of that horse himself.

Washington

Martha Washington

President Washington brought other pets to the President's House. His wife, Martha, owned a parrot named Polly. The Washingtons' children had pets too. Dogs, cats, and rabbits roamed the house.

But the president still liked Nelson best.

Blueskin and Nelson lived for many years. In 1797, Washington's term as president ended. He moved his family and animals back to Mount Vernon.

Nelson remained his special pet. George Washington continued riding horses until he died two years later.

Chapter Three

DICK

Thomas Jefferson's Mockingbird

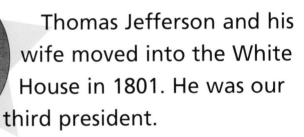

Jefferson

Thomas Jefferson and his wife moved into the White House in 1801. He was our third president.

President Jefferson loved the United States. But he did not like being president.

Jefferson did not like dressing in fancy clothes. He especially disliked going to all those meetings. He enjoyed wearing old clothes and playing with his pet bird.

Like most of the early presidents, Jefferson kept horses in the White House stables. He also had two dogs.

But President and Mrs. Jefferson loved birds. They liked walking outside the White House and watching wild birds. Jefferson wrote down the name of each bird they saw.

Thomas Jefferson had his own pet bird. It lived in a cage in his office. It was a mockingbird that Jefferson had named Dick.

Today, mockingbirds are not sold as pets. They fly freely with other wild birds. But in Jefferson's day, these birds were sold in cages. They were bought in shops just like those where we buy parakeets and canaries today.

Mockingbirds *mock*, or copy, the sounds that other birds make. Jefferson's mockingbird filled his office with all kinds of bird sounds. But Dick did more than just mock other birds. He sang!

President Jefferson always hummed while he worked. He hummed German and French folk songs. He hummed popular songs. And so did Dick. He learned the same tunes that the president hummed.

Jefferson had played the violin since he was a boy. He played when no one else was in his office. Before long, Dick would join in, singing.

Dick did not stay in the cage all the time. When the president was alone, he let Dick fly freely in the office. But most of the time, Dick did not fly. He preferred sitting on the president's shoulder.

Jefferson also let Dick help with gardening. The president kept a window box of plants by his desk. As he dug in the box, Dick hopped around in it. Sometimes the bird even pulled out weeds.

In the afternoons, the president went to his upstairs bedroom to rest. Usually he let Dick come too. Dick followed Jefferson up the steps. He hopped up one step at a time.

The president lay on the couch for a nap. Dick sat on the back of the couch. He sang the president to sleep.

At meals, President Jefferson often shared food with Dick. Dick's favorites were bread crusts and bits of fruit.

Sometimes the president held pieces of food in his mouth. Then he turned his head up. That was Dick's signal to come and get it!

Down flew Dick from the dining room curtain. He gently took the food from the president's mouth. Then he flew back to the curtain to enjoy his treat.

The Jeffersons left the White House in 1809. Thomas Jefferson was happy to have no more meetings. He finally had time to spend watching birds. He also had more time to play with Dick.

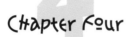

Chapter Four

NANNY and NANKO
Abraham Lincoln's
Goats

Lincoln

Abraham Lincoln became president during a difficult time in our history. It was 1861.

Mary
Lincoln

The North and South were about to fight each other in the Civil War. The only peace for Lincoln was with his family and animals.

Lincoln had grown up on a farm. Most of the animals worked in the fields. But Lincoln had one pet. It was a pig.

Lincoln and the pig grew up together. By the time he was grown, so was the pig. It was big enough for Lincoln to ride like a pony.

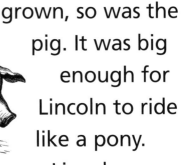

Lincoln was married when he moved into the White House. His wife, Mary, and sons, Robert, Tad and Willie, already had pets. They had a dog named Fido, two ponies, and several cats.

Willie died in 1862. Tad was very sad. People around the country tried to cheer up the Lincolns. Someone even sent Tad two white rabbits. But nothing seemed to make him happy.

One day, Lincoln and Tad were out riding. They saw some goats. Tad got very excited. Goats were popular pets at that time.

So Lincoln sent one of his helpers to buy two goats. He named them Nanny and Nanko. Tad was thrilled with the new pets.

But not everyone in the White House liked them.

Both goats got into trouble. They loved to run around the White House lawn. Most of the time, they got into the flower gardens. They

crushed some of the flowers. Then they ate the rest!

The gardener complained to

President Lincoln. He had had enough of Nanny and Nanko. Lincoln ordered that the goats be kept inside.

Tad loved playing with the goats. He put ropes and collars on them. He chased behind them. He rolled on the floor and butted heads with them.

Nanko was not as bad as Nanny. Most of the time he stayed where he was put.

But Nanny did as she pleased. She often wandered up and down the White House halls. She especially liked to curl up on Tad's bed.

For a time, the goats were good. Then one day, Tad, Nanko, and Nanny got into big trouble.

Tad pretended that he was in a race. He used a kitchen chair as his race cart. He tied Nanny and Nanko to the chair.

"Go, horses!" he shouted to the goats.

Nanny and Nanko raced out of the kitchen. They pulled Tad and the chair behind them. Tad laughed and shouted.

Lincoln was showing the White House to some ladies. They were in the East Room.

Suddenly Tad and his goats raced through the room. The women had to jump to get out of their way.

President Lincoln covered his mouth to keep from laughing. But Mrs. Lincoln did not think it was funny at all.

Finally the Lincolns gave away Nanny and Nanko. But they never forgot the goats that had brought Tad so much happiness.

Chapter Five

LADDIE BOY
Warren Harding's Dog

Warren Harding moved into the White House in 1921. He was our twenty-ninth president.

President Harding and his wife, Florence, loved animals. Mrs. Harding put up birdhouses outside the White House windows. She and President Harding enjoyed watching birds.

President Harding grew up on a farm. Even as a boy he loved dogs. He brought several with him to the White House.

The first gift he received after becoming president was a puppy. Laddie Boy was a small shaggy dog.

President Harding loved all his dogs. But Laddie Boy soon became his favorite.

The president hired Willy Jackson to take care of the puppy. Willy bathed Laddie Boy every day.

Most times, Laddie Boy stayed with President Harding. He ate parts of the president's lunch and breakfast. He also got all the dog treats he wanted.

Laddie Boy even went to important meetings. President Harding saved a special chair for his dog. He sat right beside the president.

Laddie Boy once starred in a Be Kind to Animals parade. Laddie Boy led it. He even had his very own float!

Laddie Boy liked helping President Harding. He carried newspapers to him.

When the president played golf, Laddie Boy went too. He helped find the president's golf balls.

Other times, he just went along on long walks with the president.

People from around the world sent presents to Laddie Boy. Some days, he received a sackful. People sent him sweaters and blankets. They sent balls, bones, and letters.

Once Laddie Boy had a birthday party. Other White House dogs came. So did dogs that belonged to the president's friends and neighbors.

Someone made a special birthday cake from dog biscuits. It was covered with white icing. Newspaper reporters took pictures of Laddie Boy with his cake. All the dogs had a great time at the party.

President Harding died suddenly in 1923. Mrs. Harding could not care for Laddie Boy. She gave him to a man who had worked for the president.

But people did not want to forget Laddie Boy. The Newsboys Association wanted to make a statue of him. President Harding had once worked for a newspaper. So newsboys around the country felt close to the president. They wanted the statue of Laddie Boy for Mrs. Harding.

Children from all over the United States who delivered newspapers helped. Each

 carrier sent in one penny. The pennies were used to make the statue.

Mrs. Harding died before the statue of Laddie Boy was finished. The Newsboys Association gave the statue to the Smithsonian Museum in Washington, D.C.

Visitors to the museum can see Laddie Boy's statue. It was made from gifts of love.

Chapter Six

REBECCA
Calvin Coolidge's Raccoon

Calvin Coolidge was the thirtieth president of the United States. Some people thought he was shy. That's because he did not talk or smile very much. People nicknamed him Silent Cal.

But President Coolidge was not shy around animals. He and his family probably had more animals than any other first family.

Coolidge

Coolidge had several dogs. Rob Roy, a white collie, was his favorite. Mrs. Coolidge often dressed their dogs in dresses and hats.

President Coolidge also had cats. He liked Tiger best. Tiger was a stray that just showed up one day at the White House. He liked riding up and down on the White House elevator.

The Coolidges also had a mynah bird and two canaries, Nip and Tuck.

People around the world knew of the president's love of animals. They sent him a baby bear and two lion cubs. He also received a hippo, a bobcat, and an antelope. Coolidge gave these big animals to zoos.

Grace Coolidge and her pet raccoon

But one day, he received a special gift from some friends in Mississippi. They sent him a furry raccoon. The president named her Rebecca. She became his favorite pet of all.

Rebecca was allowed to roam free. Sometimes visitors thought a wild animal had sneaked into the White House. They were surprised to learn that the raccoon was the president's pet!

At night, Rebecca slept outside. The president had a little house built just for her.

When he had time, Coolidge took Rebecca on walks. He kept her on a leash. Even on his busiest days, the president found time for Rebecca.

Rebecca loved playing in water. Coolidge made sure she always had water in her pen. He liked watching her splash. Sometimes he gave her a bar of soap. Rebecca played and made soapsuds.

Once President Coolidge and his family had to move from the White House. Workers needed to make some repairs. The animals stayed in their outside pens and houses.

But Coolidge worried about Rebecca. He was afraid she would be lonely without him. She was used to her daily walks and playtime. He also worried that she might not have enough soap to make suds.

The president could not rest. Finally, he called his driver and went to the White House. The president got out and went to Rebecca's pen. He picked her up and brought her to the car.

Coolidge took Rebecca to the zoo. He left her there to play with other raccoons until they could be together again at the White House.

When they moved back, Coolidge bought another raccoon. He named him Horace. But Rebecca did not like Horace. And Horace did not like Rebecca.

One night Horace ran away. That was all right with Rebecca. She liked being the only raccoon in the White House.

Chapter Seven

DEBBIE and BILLIE
John Kennedy's Hamsters

John F. Kennedy was the thirty-fifth president of the United States. He was much younger than most presidents. His children, Caroline and John, were young also. They had many pets.

President Kennedy's wife, Jacqueline, grew up with animals. She was an excellent horse rider. She taught Caroline and John to ride as soon as they could walk.

Kennedy

Caroline's pony was named Macaroni. Caroline won a blue ribbon while riding Macaroni when she was five years old. John's pony was Leprechaun. He learned to ride before he was two.

President and Mrs. Kennedy taught the children to take care of their ponies. The children washed and brushed them. They even cleaned their stables.

Once Macaroni trotted past Kennedy's office. The president's window was open. Macaroni stuck his head inside.

The president laughed and went back to work. Soon, Macaroni became bored and walked away.

The ponies were just two of the Kennedy White House pets. Tom Kitten and Mother Cat lived there. They stayed outside because their hair made the president sneeze.

Dogs Charlie, Clipper, Shannon, Pushinka, and Wolf ran around the White House. Charlie and Pushinka had four puppies. The White House already had too many animals. So the puppies were given away.

Charlie and Pushinka

Rabbit Zsa Zsa lived inside the White House. So did three birds. They were Robin the canary and parakeets Bluebelle and Maybelle.

Once a visitor to the White House learned how much Caroline liked the movie *Bambi*. So he sent her two deer.

President Kennedy let the deer stay. They lived outside on the lawn. But they began to eat the flowers and bushes. So Kennedy gave them to a zoo.

Of all the Kennedy pets, Debbie and Billie became the best known. Those two hamsters got into all kinds of trouble! They always found ways to get out of their cage. Newspaper reporters loved writing stories about them.

The hamsters often got lost. The White House had many places for them to hide.

Debbie and Billie popped up in funny places. They could be behind a curtain or in someone's shoe. They made nests and had babies in cozy places.

Sometimes the hamsters got sick. Once a newspaper printed a story when Billie had a cold. He had fallen into a bathtub full of water. Poor Billie was not used to being wet. He sneezed and coughed for days.

Billie and Debbie fought with each other just like some brothers and sisters. When reporters asked about the hamsters, Kennedy would just shake his head and laugh.

Hamsters do not live for a long time. By the time Lyndon Johnson became president, Billie and Debbie had died.

Some of Billie and Debbie's children probably moved out with the Kennedys. But who knows? Some might have stayed hidden in the White House.

Chapter Eight

SOCKS
William Clinton's Cat

The Clinton family moved into the White House in 1993. William Clinton became the forty-second president.

At that time, the president had only one pet. This was a black and white cat named Socks.

Socks had mostly black hair with splashes of white. He was not a fancy cat. But Socks was popular with people. This might have been because he looked so ordinary.

The Clintons had found Socks when they lived in Arkansas. They adopted him in 1991. He did not know then how famous he would become.

News reporters loved Socks. His picture and stories about him appeared in newspapers and on television. Visitors to the White House always hoped to see him. But Socks did not always stay at the White House.

Mrs. Clinton took him to hospitals to visit sick people. She took him to schools and children's homes. Socks rode in his own carrying case inside the president's car.

Hillary Clinton and Socks at the
Children's National Medical Center

Soon, Socks began receiving sacks of mail. Children wrote him letters. They sent pictures of their cats and dogs. They asked for pictures of Socks.

The Clintons did not have time to answer all the letters. And Socks liked sleeping better than opening his mail.

So some older people at a nearby nursing home helped. They opened Socks' mail and wrote his letters for him. They mailed out pictures of Socks to everyone who asked for them.

Socks was happy that all these people helped. He often visited them. He liked sitting on the letters after the people opened them.

Socks always got lots of petting and hugs at the nursing home. He gave kitty hugs too.

Socks liked playing around the White House. He enjoyed visiting the president's secretary. He often sat on her desk. Sometimes he got into the president's office.

Clinton

Socks took walks with President and Mrs. Clinton. Sometimes he sat on the president's shoulder and let the president do the walking. He also enjoyed catching bugs. His favorites were spiders.

Four years after moving to the White House, President Clinton got a puppy. He named it Buddy.

Everyone worried about Socks. Would he be happy to

Bill Clinton and Buddy

share the White House with another pet? Would he be angry? Would Buddy and Socks like each other?

Socks decided that he would just pretend Buddy was not there. Most of the time they stayed out of each other's way.

Hillary Clinton and the book about Socks and Buddy

Before leaving the White House, President Clinton's wife, Hillary, wrote a book. It was all about Socks and Buddy. She put in many of the children's letters to the White House pets.

One letter was to Socks from a boy named Chris. It asked, "Do you like Buddy? Don't feel bad, because they still love you."

And it was true. The Clintons had plenty of love for both presidential pets.

Fun Facts about Presidential Pets

Many presidents have lived in the White House. So have many pets. Funny and strange things happened with so many animals meeting so many people. Here are a few more presidential pet "tails."

President Theodore Roosevelt had a dog named Pete. It liked to chew. Once, Pete chewed a hole in the pants of a very important visitor from France!

President McKinley had a talking parrot. It sang "America" and "Yankee Doodle." When women passed the cage, it screamed, "Look at all the pretty girls!"

President George Bush wrote a book about being president (1989–1993). Mrs. Bush wrote a book about their dog, Millie. It told what it was like to be a dog living in the White House. The book about Millie sold more copies than the book about President Bush!

President John Kennedy taught his dog Pushinka to climb a ladder. The dog could then climb up into Caroline Kennedy's tree house.

Once President Franklin D. Roosevelt took his dog, Fala, on a trip to an island. On the way home, he noticed Fala had been left behind. He sent a Navy ship back to pick up the dog!

Roosevelt and Fala

President Andrew Jackson bought his wife a parrot. The parrot lived longer than the president or Mrs. Jackson. Someone brought the parrot to President Jackson's funeral. Everyone laughed when the parrot shouted out some bad words in the middle of the service.

President William Clinton named his puppy Buddy. He chose that name because he had an uncle Buddy.

The president's uncle had raised dogs for 50 years. Clinton wanted to honor his uncle by naming the dog for him.

President Benjamin Harrison had a goat named His Whiskers. He let the goat pull his grandchildren around in a cart.

One day His Whiskers ran through the White House gate pulling the cart behind him. President Harrison chased the goat cart through the streets of Washington!

President Herbert Hoover had ten dogs in the White House. His favorite was King Tut.

King Tut was a German shepherd. Before becoming president, Hoover had posters made of himself with King Tut. He thought that more people would  vote for him if they saw he loved dogs. And he was right!

 Other unusual White House pets have included a horned toad, silkworms, and a kangaroo rat.

Future presidents will most likely have pets. What might the next presidential pets be? Only time will tell. But whatever these first pets are, writers and television reporters will be sure to tell Americans plenty of new presidential "pet tails."